Overview Traveling Around the City

Jacinta and her sister explore the city.

Reading Vocabulary Words

fuel
vehicle
adults

High-Frequency Words

on	can
our	some
city	us
are	car

Building Future Vocabulary

* These vocabulary words do not appear in this text. They are provided to develop related oral vocabulary that first appears in future texts.

Words:	sufficient	commute	efficient
Levels:	Library	Library	Library

Comprehension Strategy
Using text features and structures to determine importance

Fluency Skill
Taking a breath at appropriate times

Phonics Skill
Reading more complex and irregularly spelled words (Jacinta, bicycle, exercise, route, fuel, stations)

Reading-Writing Connection
Making a chart

Home Connection
Send home one of the Flying Colors Take-Home books for children to share with their families.

Differentiated Instruction
Before reading the text, query children to discover their level of understanding of the comprehension strategy — Using text features and structures to determine importance. As you work together, provide additional support to children who show a beginning mastery of the strategy.

Focus on ELL
- Have children name the different ways they have traveled. Write the list on the board and help children associate the words with the correct English terms.

- Have children share their personal experiences of riding in different kinds of vehicles.

T1

Using This Teaching Version

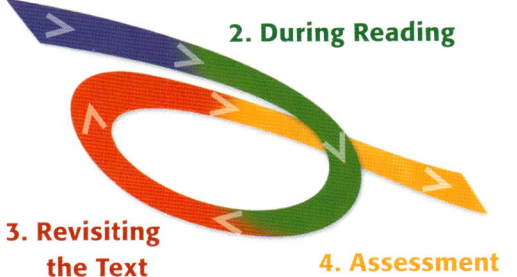

1. Before Reading
2. During Reading
3. Revisiting the Text
4. Assessment

This Teaching Version will assist you in directing children through the process of reading.

1. **Begin with Before Reading** to familiarize children with the book's content. Select the skills and strategies that meet the needs of your children.

2. **Next, go to During Reading** to help children become familiar with the text, and then to read individually on their own.

3. **Then, go back to Revisiting the Text** and select those specific activities that meet children's needs.

4. **Finally, finish with Assessment** to confirm children are ready to move forward to the next text.

1 Before Reading

Building Background

- Write the word *vehicle* on the board. Read it aloud. Ask children to share the different kinds of vehicles in which they have ridden. Have them share which ones are their favorites and why.

- Introduce the book by reading the title, talking about the cover photograph, and sharing the overview.

Building Future Vocabulary
Use Interactive Modeling Card: Meaning Map

- Write *commute* in the Word box. In the Sentence box, write a sentence using the word.

- Ask children what they think the word means and record their responses.

- Together with children, look up the definition of *commute* and write it on the card. Have children create a new sentence using the word and write it on the card.

Introduction to Reading Vocabulary

- On blank cards write: *fuel*, *vehicle*, and *adults*. Read them aloud. Tell children these words will appear in the text of *Traveling Around the City.*

- Use each word in a sentence for understanding.

Introduction to Comprehension Strategy

- Explain that books, especially nonfiction, often use special text features and different text structures to help the reader find important information.
- Tell children that they will be examining text features and structures as they read *Traveling Around the City.*
- Point to the cover and ask children what special features are used to highlight the title. (larger text, colored text, and outlined letters)

Introduction to Phonics

- Write **Jacinta** on the board. Read it aloud and have children repeat the name after you. Say *This is the name of a girl in the book. Names often have unique spellings.*
- Explain that when encountering a complex or unusually spelled word, it helps to sound it out.
- Ask children for other unique names and list them on the board. Have children practice reading aloud the names on the board.

Modeling Fluency

- Read aloud page 2, modeling taking a breath after the first sentence and the last sentence.
- Point out that it is appropriate to pause and take a breath after a period.

2 During Reading

Book Talk

Beginning on page T4, use the During Reading notes on the left-hand side to engage children in a book talk. On page 24, follow with *Individual Reading.*

During Reading

Book Talk
- If children do not live in a big city, ask them if they have ever been to a city and have them share their experiences. If children live in a big city, ask them what their favorite part of the city is and have them share their experiences.

- **Comprehension Strategy**
Ask *Which text stands out the most in the table of contents?* (the book title and the chapter titles) *Why is this text highlighted?* (It is the most important information on the page.)

Turn to page 2 – Book Talk

Revisiting the Text

Traveling Around the City

Julie Haydon

Chapter 1	A Week in the City	2
Chapter 2	An Airplane Trip	4
Chapter 3	Aunt Clare's Car	7
Chapter 4	Biking to Grandpa's	10
Chapter 5	A Bus Ride	13
Chapter 6	The Ferry	16
Chapter 7	On the Train	19
Chapter 8	Other Vehicles	22
Glossary and Index		24

Future Vocabulary

- Ask *Do you think the chapter titles provide a sufficient amount of information about each chapter's topic?*

- Say *Most of the vehicles mentioned in the book can be used by people to commute, or travel to work in the morning. Which vehicle is not likely to be used for daily commuting?* (airplane)

Now revisit pages 2–3

During Reading

Book Talk

- **Comprehension Strategy**
  Ask *Which text on these pages appears to be the least important?* (the caption to the drawing) *How can you tell?* (It is smaller and near the bottom of the page.)

- **Fluency Skill** Read page 3, modeling taking a breath after the first sentence. Have children raise their hands when you take a breath. Ask *Why did I take a breath before the second sentence?* (because the second sentence is long)

Turn to page 4 – Book Talk

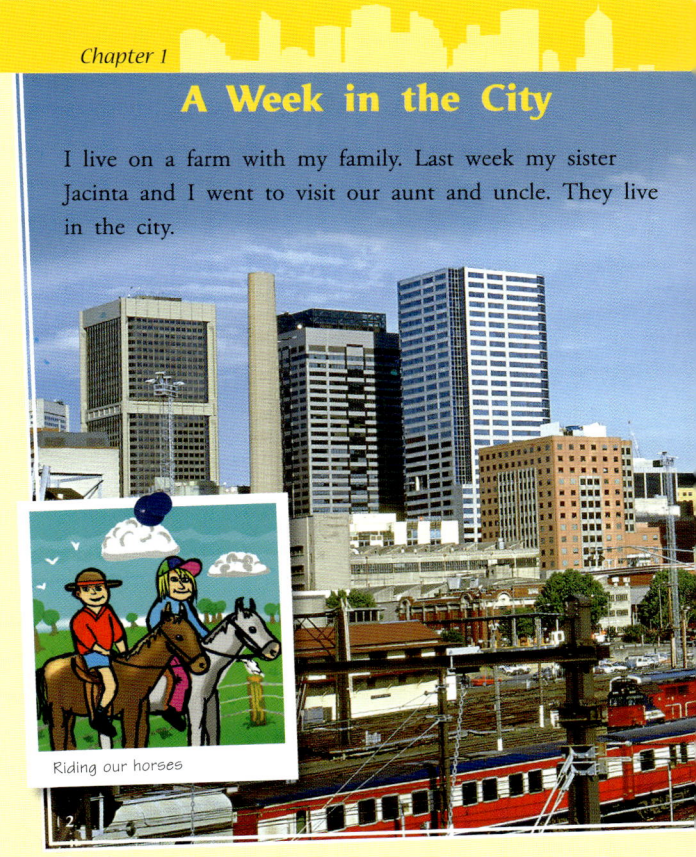

Revisiting the Text

The city is big. Jacinta and I used different kinds of **transportation** to get around. It was easy and fun.

Future Vocabulary
- Say *These trains are called passenger trains because they carry people and not cargo. They are also sometimes called commuter trains because people use them to commute to and from the city.*

Now revisit pages 4–5

During Reading

Book Talk

- **Comprehension Strategy**
  Explain that when talking about importance, we sometimes say something is of primary importance or secondary importance. Explain that *primary* means most important and *secondary* means less important. Ask *On page 4, which text is of secondary importance?* (the labels on the photograph of the airplane)

- Ask *How is the information on page 5 organized?* (in a chart) *Which text on the chart is most important?* (the title and the column headings) *How can you tell?* (The title is big and white and at the very top of the chart; the column headings are bold and near the top.) *Why is this text important?* (It tells what the chart is about and how to read the chart.)

Turn to page 6 — Book Talk

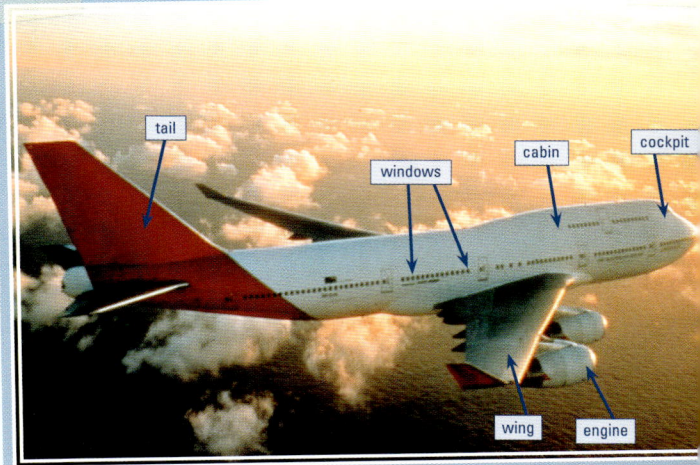

Chapter 2

An Airplane Trip

On Sunday Jacinta and I went to the airport. We flew to the city on an airplane.

4

Revisiting the Text

Airplanes	
Airplanes are good because:	Airplanes are bad because:
They are fast.	They make the air dirty.
They can travel short or long distances.	They are noisy.
They can carry lots of people.	Airplane tickets can be expensive.

Flying in an airplane

Future Vocabulary
- Point to the photograph on page 4. Ask *Do you think the labels provide a sufficient amount of information about the airplane's different parts?*

- Say *Some forms of transportation are more efficient than others. Do you think the large airplanes on pages 4–5 are an efficient way to move large numbers of people long distances? Why or why not?* (Yes, large airplanes can move many people a long distance in a short time.)

Now revisit pages 6–7

5

During Reading

Book Talk

- **Fluency Skill** Read page 6 aloud, modeling taking a breath at appropriate times. Direct children to raise their hands when you take a breath.

- Point out the photograph at the bottom of page 6 and ask children if they know what kind of ship it is. (aircraft carrier) Explain that it allows airplanes to take off and land in remote, faraway places or in the middle of the ocean. Point out that only small airplanes can take off and land on an aircraft carrier.

Turn to page 8 — Book Talk

Some airplanes carry only a **pilot**. Other airplanes can carry hundreds of passengers. Some airplanes carry **goods**.

Most airplanes land on the ground, but some land on water. Other airplanes can land on small spaces, such as ships.

Revisiting the Text

Chapter 3

Aunt Clare's Car

Aunt Clare met us at the airport. She drove us to her house in her car.

Future Vocabulary

- Ask *Which of the vehicles on pages 6–7 would be the most efficient way to travel across town?* (the car)

Now revisit pages 8–9

During Reading

Book Talk
- Have children locate the word *adults* on page 8. Ask *What are some other big things that adults can buy?* (truck, house, boat)
- **Fluency Skill** Ask volunteers to read page 9 aloud. Have children raise their hands when the reader takes a breath. If the reader breathes at an inappropriate spot, point out a better place in the text for taking a breath.

Turn to page 10 — Book Talk

Cars	
Cars are good because:	Cars are bad because:
They make it easy for people to travel.	They make the air dirty.
Most **adults** can buy and own a car.	They are noisy.
Many cars can carry at least five people.	Sometimes people are hurt in car accidents.
	Parking lots take up a lot of space.

Traveling in Aunt Clare's car

Revisiting the Text

Lots of people drive cars every day. Most cars are driven on roads. Many cars usually carry between two and five passengers.

Some people use their cars for work.

Other cars are used in sports, such as car racing.

Future Vocabulary

- Point to the photograph on page 8. Say *Because so many people* commute *into big cities for work, there are often traffic jams in the mornings and evenings. Sometimes this time of day is called rush hour. If you are planning to drive into the city during rush hour, you need to allow a* sufficient *amount of time to get through traffic.* Allow children to share their experiences with traffic jams.

Now revisit pages 10–11

During Reading

Book Talk

- Have children locate the word *vehicles* on page 11. Review with children the *vehicles* that have been mentioned so far in the book. (airplane, car, bicycle)

- **Phonics Skill** Have children locate the words *bicycle* and *exercise* on these pages. Write the words on the board and draw slashes between the syllables. Have children read the words aloud slowly while you trace your finger beneath each syllable.

- Ask children to examine the photograph of the bike and name some of the parts that are not labeled. (brakes, reflectors, water bottle, kickstand)

Turn to page 12 – Book Talk

Chapter 4

Biking to Grandpa's

On Monday Jacinta and I went to visit Grandpa. We rode bicycles to his house.

handlebars · seat · frame · pedal · tire · chain · spokes · wheel

10

Revisiting the Text

Bicycles

Bicycles are good because:	Bicycles are bad because:
They are not too expensive.	They are not as fast as other **vehicles**.
They do not make the air dirty.	The rider can get tired.
They are not noisy.	The rider is not safe from bad weather.
Children and adults can ride bicycles.	
Bicycle riding is good exercise.	

Biking to Grandpa's house

Future Vocabulary

- Say *Some people who live near their workplace commute by bike instead of by car.*
- Ask *Why is riding a bicycle a more efficient way to travel short distances than a car?* (Bicycles do not use gas.)

Now revisit pages 12–13

11

During Reading

Book Talk

- **Comprehension Strategy** Ask *Which text on these pages is of secondary importance?* (the chapter number and the bus labels) *Which text is of primary importance?* (the chapter title) *Why do you think the chapter title is more important than the chapter number?* (The title gives information about the chapter.)

- **Fluency Skill** Point to the last paragraph on page 12. Ask *Where is the best place in this paragraph to take a breath?* (after the second sentence) *Why?* (It is in the middle of the paragraph; it is at a period; it is before the longest sentence in the paragraph.)

Turn to page 14 – Book Talk

Some people ride bicycles to school and work. Some people ride bicycles for fun or to keep fit.

Many bicycles are ridden on roads. Other bicycles are ridden on dirt. Some bicycles are ridden on special racetracks. Some people ride in bicycle races.

Revisiting the Text

Chapter 5

A Bus Ride

On Tuesday Uncle Andrew took us to the movies. We rode on a bus to the theater.

Future Vocabulary

- Say *Bicycles and buses are efficient ways to travel in a city. When might a bus be a more efficient way to travel than a bicycle?* (The weather is bad; you need to carry something; you have to travel a long distance.)

Now revisit pages 14–15

During Reading

Book Talk

- **Phonics Skill** Have children locate the word *route* on page 15. Say *Some words can be pronounced more than one way. This word can be pronounced like a tree root* (/root/) *or like the word* out (/rowt/). Have volunteers take turns reading the sentence aloud.

- Point to the photograph at the top of page 15. Say *The man in the wheelchair is using a special device to board the bus. Do you know what it is called?* (a lift) *What other devices help people in wheelchairs get around?* (ramps, elevators)

Turn to page 16 — Book Talk

| Buses ||
Buses are good because:	Buses are bad because:
Bus tickets are not too expensive.	People cannot choose where the bus goes.
They can take people on short or long trips.	They are noisy.
Lots of people ride in buses instead of driving cars. This means fewer cars on the roads and less dirty air.	They make the air dirty.

Riding on the bus

Revisiting the Text

Buses travel on roads. Most buses follow a **route**. People get on and off the bus at bus stops.

Sometimes buses are used to take people on trips. School buses carry children to and from school.

Future Vocabulary
- Say *Because buses are so long and make wide turns, they need to have sufficient space to make a turn. What other kinds of vehicles make wide turns?* (big trucks, boats, airplanes)

Now revisit pages 16–17

15

During Reading

Book Talk

- **Comprehension Strategy** Ask *What is the most important text on page 17?* (the chart title and column headings)

- Ask children if they have ever ridden on a ferry and have them share their experiences.

- Have children examine the photograph on page 17 and locate the ferry's features that are labeled on page 16.

Turn to page 18 – Book Talk

Revisiting the Text

Ferries	
Ferries are good because:	Ferries are bad because:
They travel over water.	They can move up and down if there are lots of waves. This can make people sick.
They carry lots of passengers.	They make the air and water dirty.
Some ferries carry cars as well as people.	

Our ferry trip

Future Vocabulary
- Say *In cities that are by water, some people commute to work on a ferry.*
- Ask *When might riding a ferry be a more efficient way to cross water than driving a car over a bridge?* (when the bridge has heavy traffic; when you need to cross to a point that is far from the bridge)

Now revisit pages 18–19

During Reading

Book Talk

- Point to the photograph at the top of page 18. Ask *How is this ferry different from the ferries on the previous pages?* (The middle of the hull is above the water.)

- Review the train labels on page 19. Say *On a train they call the driver the engineer. The engineer starts and stops the train and controls the train's speed.*

Turn to page 20 – Book Talk

Ferries can be different sizes. Some small ferries make short trips. These ferries take people to work or to school or on short trips.

Other big ferries make longer trips. Sometimes people sleep in bedrooms on these ferries.

Revisiting the Text

Future Vocabulary

- Say *Ships that go on long trips must bring along sufficient supplies to last for the journey. What kinds of supplies would be needed on a long trip?* Accept all reasonable responses.

Now revisit pages 20–21

During Reading

Book Talk

- **Phonics Skill** Have children locate the words *fuel* and *stations* on these pages. Say *Sometimes people refer to a gas station as a fueling station.* Write *fueling station* on the board. Have children read aloud as you trace your finger beneath the words.

- Ask *What are trains that travel underground sometimes called?* (subways) Have children share their experiences with subways.

Turn to page 22 — Book Talk

Trains	
Trains are good because:	Trains are bad because:
Train tickets are not too expensive.	People cannot choose where the train goes.
They can carry lots of passengers on short or long trips.	They use **fuel**. This makes the air dirty.
Lots of people ride in trains instead of driving cars. This means fewer cars on the roads and less dirty air.	
They have their own tracks.	
They can be very fast.	

20   Riding on the train

20

Revisiting the Text

Passengers get on and off trains at stations. Some trains travel in tunnels under the ground. Some trains travel above the ground.

Passenger trains carry people. Other trains carry goods.

Future Vocabulary
- Point to the illustration at the bottom of page 20. Say *This train must draw a sufficient amount of energy from the wires in order to move. What kind of energy runs through these wires?* (electricity)

Now revisit pages 22–23

During Reading

Book Talk
- Leave this page spread for children to discover on their own when they read the book individually.

Turn to page 24 – Book Talk

Chapter 8

Other Vehicles

On Friday Aunt Clare drove us to the airport. Jacinta and I were going home. Our week in the city was fun!

Here are some other vehicles we saw in the city.

a horse and carriage

a motorcycle

22

Revisiting the Text

a fire engine

a helicopter

Future Vocabulary

- Ask *Which one of these vehicles do news stations use in the mornings to describe the commuter traffic?* (the helicopter) *Why do they use a helicopter?* (It can see the traffic from high above.)

- Ask *Which of the vehicles on pages 22–23 would be the least efficient way to travel a long distance?* (the horse and carriage)

Go to page T5 – Revisiting the Text

During Reading

Book Talk

- Note: Point out this text feature page as a reference for children's use while reading independently.

Individual Reading

Have each child read the entire book at his or her own pace while remaining in the group.

*Go to page T5 —
Revisiting the Text*

Glossary

adults	people who are grown up
expensive	costing a lot of money
fuel	something that is burned to make power or heat
goods	things people own
pilot	a person who flies an airplane
route	a way that is taken all the time
transportation	a way of getting from place to place
vehicles	kinds of transportation

Index

airport 7, 22
airplanes 4–6
bicycles 10–12
buses 13–15
bus stops 15
cars 7–9

exercise 11
ferries 16–18
goods 6, 21
passengers 6, 9, 17, 21
stations 21
trains 19–21

24

 During independent work time, children can read the online book at:
www.rigbyflyingcolors.com

3 Revisiting the Text

Future Vocabulary
- Use the notes on the right-hand pages to develop oral vocabulary that goes beyond the text. These vocabulary words first appear in future texts. These words are: *sufficient*, *commute*, and *efficient*.

Turn back to page 1

Reading Vocabulary Review
Activity Sheet: Same and Opposite

- Have children write the word *adults* in the top box.
- Tell children to list words with the same meaning as *adults* in the box on the left and words that mean the opposite in the box on the right.

Comprehension Strategy Review
Use Interactive Modeling Card: Text Connections Web

- Write *Traveling Around the City* in the center box. Explain to children that all of the categories listed at the top of the card are types of connections that they might have to the story.
- Discuss connections for each category with children and list responses in the boxes.

Phonics Review
- Remind children that complex or irregularly spelled words can be pronounced by sounding out the individual syllables.
- Have children read aloud the first column of the chart on page 11.

Fluency Review
- Remind children to take a breath at periods and before long sentences when reading aloud.
- Read aloud pages 2–3, modeling taking a breath at appropriate times.

Reading-Writing Connection
Activity Sheet: Making Your Own Judgment

To assist children with linking reading and writing:

- Have children review *Traveling Around the City* and choose three facts from the charts in the book to write in the Nonfiction Fact column.
- In the second column, tell children to write a judgment based on each fact. In the last column, have children write an explanation or additional detail from the book that supports their judgment.
- Have children choose a form of transportation not discussed in the book and create their own chart listing its good things and bad things.

4 Assessment

Assessing Future Vocabulary

Work with each child individually. Ask questions that elicit each child's understanding of the Future Vocabulary words. Note each child's responses:

- What kind of vehicle would be sufficient to carry 20 people?
- What are three ways that people commute to work?
- Which is a more efficient way to get a large number of children to school, ride together in a school bus or ride separately in cars?

Assessing Comprehension Strategy

Work with each child individually. Note each child's understanding of using text features and structures to determine importance:

- What are some special features that indicate important text?
- In a chart, where do you place important information such as the chart title?
- If information is less important, how might that be reflected in the text?

Assessing Phonics

Work with each child individually. Write the words *Jacinta, bicycle, exercise,* and *stations* on the board. Have each child draw a slash between the syllables of each word and read each word aloud. Note each child's responses for reading more complex and irregularly spelled words:

- Did each child correctly divide the words into syllables?
- Did each child accurately pronounce each word?
- Did each child read the words easily and smoothly?

Assessing Fluency

Have each child read page 6 to you. Note each child's understanding of taking a breath at appropriate times:

- Was each child able to read through the text smoothly without losing breath?
- Did each child breathe at appropriate places?
- Did each child try to breathe at periods and before long sentences, and avoid breathing at commas and in the middle of sentences?

Interactive Modeling Cards

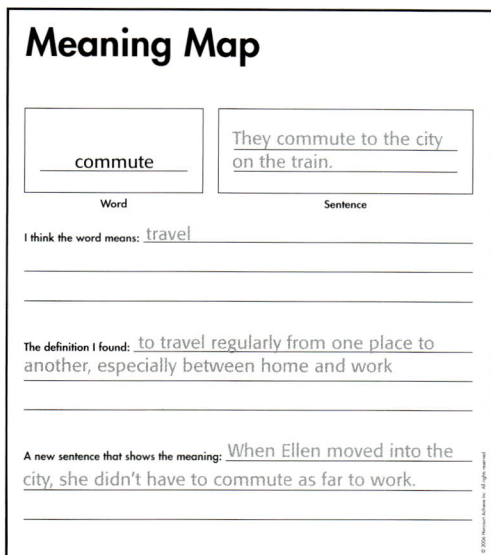

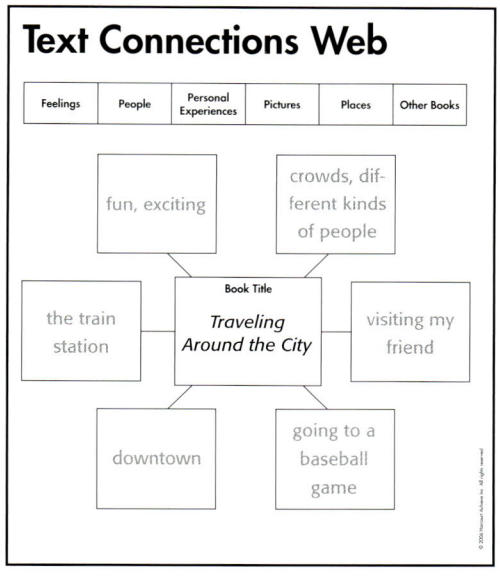

Directions: With children, fill in the Meaning Map using the word *commute*.

Directions: With children, fill in the Text Connections Web for *Traveling Around the City*.

Discussion Questions

- On what kind of boat do people commute to work? (Literal)
- How do cars and other vehicles pollute the environment? (Critical Thinking)
- Why is it less expensive to take a bus than an airplane? (Inferential)

T7

Activity Sheets

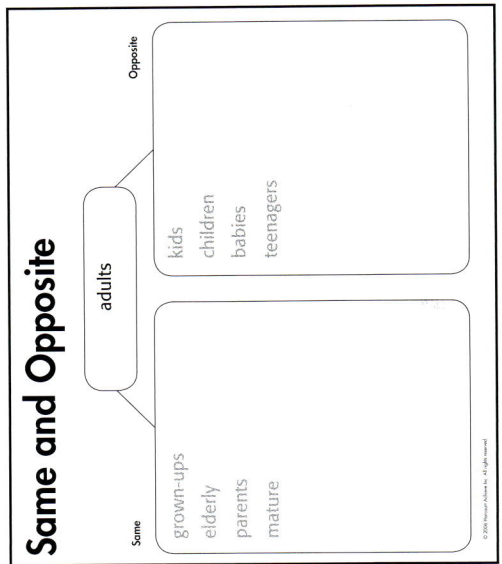

Directions: Have children fill in the Same and Opposite chart using the word *adults*.

Directions: Have children fill in the Making Your Own Judgment chart for *Traveling Around the City*.

Optional: On a separate sheet of paper, have children make a chart of advantages and disadvantages for another form of transportation.